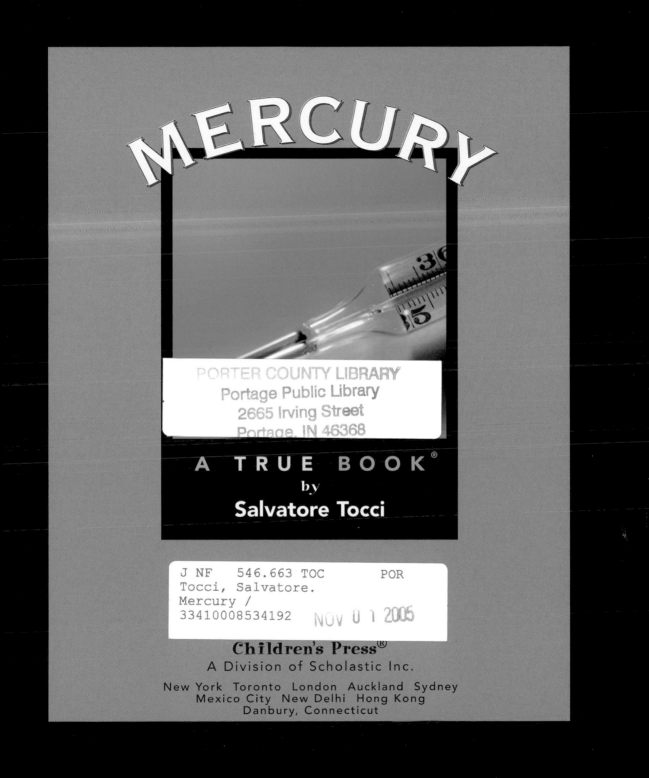

MERCURY

A TRUE BOOK®

by

Salvatore Tocci

Children's Press®
A Division of Scholastic Inc.

New York Toronto London Auckland Sydney
Mexico City New Delhi Hong Kong
Danbury, Connecticut

Mercury is
sometimes
called
quicksilver.

Reading Consultant
Julia McKenzie Munemo, MEd
New York, New York

Science Consultant
John A. Benner
Austin, Texas

*The photo on the cover shows drops
of mercury. The photo on the title
page shows the tip of a thermometer.*

*The author and the publisher are not
responsible for injuries or accidents
that occur during or from any
experiments. Experiments should be
conducted in the presence of or with
the help of an adult. Any instructions
of the experiments that require the
use of sharp, hot, or other unsafe
items should be conducted by or
with the help of an adult.*

Library of Congress Cataloging-in-Publication Data

Tocci, Salvatore.
    Mercury / by Salvatore Tocci.
    p. cm. — (A true book)
    Includes bibliographical references and index.
    ISBN 0-516-23700-4 (lib. bdg.)   0-516-25576-2 (pbk.)
    1. Mercury—Juvenile literature. I. Title. II. Series.
QD181.H6T63 2005
546'.663—dc22   2004027154

Contents

1. What did the dentist say
   when his wife baked a cake?

2. What belongs to you but others use
   it more often than you do?

3. The more of them you take,
   the more you leave behind.
   What are they?

4. What comes once in a minute,
   twice in a moment, but never
   in a thousand years?

How many of these riddles can you
answer? You can find the answers
in the Important Words section.

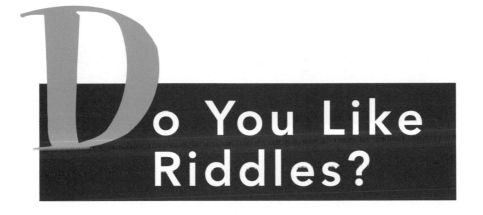

Do You Like Riddles?

When is the last time you heard a riddle that made you laugh? The funniest riddles sometimes have answers that are made-up words that sound like real words. For example, how do rabbits like to travel? (By hareplane). Other riddles are funny because the answers are real words that have no connection to the question. For example, what kind of food do racehorses like? (Fast food).

If you have read the book *Alice's Adventures in Wonderland*, you may remember a character named the Mad Hatter who asked Alice a riddle at a tea party. The Mad Hatter asked, "Why is a raven like a writing desk?" When Alice could not figure out why, she asked the Mad Hatter for the answer. He replied that he did not know the answer.

Asking riddles with no answer was not the only odd behavior of the Mad Hatter. This character got his name from an expression that was first used to describe workers who made felt hats in the 1800s. Some of these hats were made with rabbit fur. The fur was brushed with a substance that gave off fumes.

People who made felt hats such as these sometimes became mad hatters.

With little ventilation to bring in fresh air, the workers were constantly breathing in these fumes. After breathing in these fumes for some time, these workers started to behave very strangely. People soon started using the expression "mad as a hatter."

What caused these workers to become mad hatters? It was a substance called mercury.

What Is Mercury?

Mercury is an **element**. An element is the building block of **matter**. Matter is the stuff or material that makes up everything in the universe. This book, the chair you are sitting on, and even your body are all made of matter.

10

There are millions of different kinds of matter. There are just a few more than one hundred different elements. So how can so many different kinds of matter be made up of so few elements?

Just compare the many kinds of matter to the English language. All of the words in the language can be made with the twenty-six letters of the alphabet. The elements

The liquid in this bottle contains mercury. In the past, it was applied to cuts on the skin to help prevent infections.

are like these letters. Though there are just over one hundred elements, they can be combined in many different ways to make all of the matter in the universe.

Making Crystals

You can use the mercury compound merbromin to help you grow crystals. The merbromin will make the crystals colorful. Ask an adult to help you break a piece of charcoal into small lumps. Place the lumps around the bottom of a glass jar. In another glass jar, mix 2 tablespoons each of salt, ammonia, and water. Pour this solution over the lumps. Scatter 10 drops of merbromin over the top. Place the jar in a location where it won't be disturbed. Observe the jar each day. In a few days, you should see crystals beginning to grow.

Like most other elements, mercury is a metal. The one property that all metals share is their ability to allow electricity to pass through them. Metals are good **conductors** of electricity. Mercury, however, is not as good a conductor as many other metals, such as silver and copper.

In the middle of the eighteenth century, only seven metals were known. By coincidence, only seven planets

If you dropped a thermometer such as this one, the mercury would form shiny beads. Trying to pick up these beads would be dangerous. So if you ever see a mercury spill, find an adult who can clean it up safely.

were known at that time. It seemed natural to name a metal after one of the planets. The element mercury was named after the planet Mercury.

At that time, scientists observed that the planet Mercury moves somewhat differently from other planets as it orbits the Sun. They could not explain this unusual movement. They also observed that the element mercury behaved somewhat differently. Unlike

The element mercury was named after the planet Mercury.

Mercury (above) and bromine
are the only two elements that
are liquid at room temperature.

the other six metals known at that time, mercury exists as a liquid, not as a solid, at room temperature. Scientists could not explain this unusual property either. Because of their unusual characteristics, the element and the planet came to share the same name.

Every element has both a name and a symbol made up of one, two, or three letters. The symbol for mercury is Hg. This symbol comes from *hydragyrum*, which is Latin for "water silver." This Latin name reflected the fact that at room temperature, mercury is a liquid that has a silver color.

The Latin-speaking early Romans, however, were not the first people to use mercury. Objects containing mercury have been found in Egyptian tombs that are more than five thousand years old. The Egyptians used a substance that contained mercury as a

An ancient Greek physician treats a patient. In ancient Greece, mercury was sometimes used as a medicine.

ΙΑϹΩΝΟΚΑΙΔΕΚΜΟϹΑΧΑΡΝΕΥϹΙΑΤΡΟϹ
ΔΙΟΝΥϹΙΟϹΙΑϹΟΝΟϹΑΧΑΡΓΟΝΩΔΕΘΕΟΔΩΡΟΥΑϹΜΟΝΕΩ

cosmetic. In addition, the ancient Greeks used mercury as a medicine. These people did not know how dangerous mercury is.

Why Is Mercury Dangerous?

As a liquid, the element mercury is not dangerous. Even if it is accidentally swallowed, the mercury will not cause any poisoning in a healthy person. The mercury will simply pass through the stomach and out of the body. Even touching

A person is most likely to come into contact with mercury from a broken thermometer. Only thermometers with a silver-colored line contain mercury.

liquid mercury for a short time is not dangerous, as long as a person does not do it often. Mercury does not pass through the skin very easily.

Mercury, however, is dangerous when it is inhaled through the lungs. Mercury slowly **vaporizes**, or turns into a gas, at room temperature. A person can then inhale the mercury vapors or fumes. A short, one-time exposure to mercury vapors is not likely to cause problems. If the exposure is large enough or long enough, however, a person can develop mercury poisoning.

Mercury can also be dangerous when it is part of a compound. A compound is a substance that is made when two or more different elements combine to form a single substance. For example, mercury can combine with an element called sulfur. The compound they form is called

When mercury combines with sulfur, it forms cinnabar, a compound with a bright red color.

mercuric sulfide, which is also known as cinnabar.

If mercury gets into a person's body, it can damage the

kidneys and destroy nerves. The people who made felt hats in the 1800s became poisoned by the dust and vapors given off by a mercury compound. Damage to their nerves caused them to be confused and suffer memory loss.

The most dangerous mercury compounds are formed when the metal combines with an element called carbon. One example of such a compound is methylmercury. This

A small amount of mercury is released into the air when a volcano erupts.

compound can be created when mercury from the air is deposited on land or in water.

Microorganisms then change the mercury into methylmercury. This compound enters rivers, lakes and other bodies of water. It builds up in the bodies of fish and shellfish. Animals that eat these contaminated fish and shellfish can become sick.

Fish that have been found to contain high levels of mercury include swordfish, tuna, and sharks. Humans who eat these fish are the next in line to take in methylmercury. This mercury compound can attack every part of a person's body. It is especially dangerous to babies.

How does mercury get into the air to begin this cycle of poisoning? Most of the mercury in the air comes from coal burning power plants. The improper disposal of products containing mercury and the burning of dangerous wastes are other ways that mercury enters our environment.

How Is Mercury Useful?

Mercury is useful as an element in several ways. Many thermometers measure temperature with the help of mercury that is sealed inside a glass tube. The thin column of mercury rises and falls with changes in temperature.

For safety reasons, mercury thermometers have been replaced in homes and schools with ones that use alcohol colored with a red dye.

Mercury is also used in barometers that measure changes in air pressure.

Because it conducts electricity, mercury is used in batteries and electrical switches. An electrical switch consists of a small tube that contains mercury. When the tube tilts one way, the liquid mercury collects at one end. The mercury completes the electrical circuit and turns on the switch. When the tube

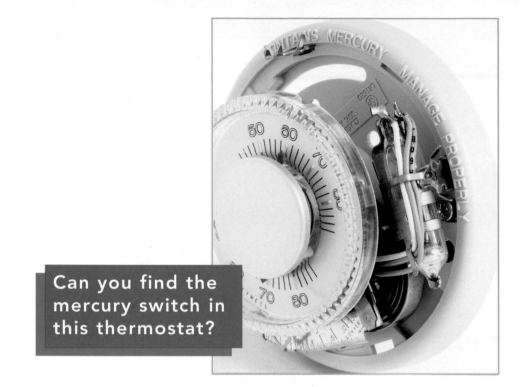

Can you find the
mercury switch in
this thermostat?

tilts in the opposite direction,
the mercury collects at the
other end. This shifting of the
mercury breaks the electrical
circuit and turns off the switch.
Mercury switches are sometimes used in thermostats.

Turning On and Off

See how a mercury switch operates. Ask an adult to help you remove the cover from a thermostat that has a mercury switch. You may have one at home. If not, you can buy an inexpensive one at a hardware or home supply store. If you buy one, mount it on a board as you would on a wall. Locate the mercury switch and the metal coil that are inside the thermostat. Blow hot air from a hair dryer on the metal coil. Watch what happens to the mercury switch. Next blow cool air on the metal coil and watch what happens to the switch. Can you explain how the switch works?

Mercury is also used in lights known as mercury vapor lamps. These lamps produce a very bright light for outdoor use on streets and in parking lots, and for indoor use in gymnasiums and factories. Not only do they give off much brighter light than ordinary lightbulbs do, mercury vapor lamps also use less energy and last much longer.

Compounds that contain mercury are useful as well.

A mercury compound is used to set off dynamite.

Cinnabar, for example, was used by ancient Egyptians as a cosmetic. Though cinnabar is no longer used as a cosmetic because of the mercury it contains, it is still used as a source for the mercury needed for thermometers and other devices. Other mercury compounds are used to kill germs, insects, and rats.

Mercury can also be mixed with other metals to make an **amalgam**. Tooth cavities are

often filled with dental amalgams, which are commonly
called fillings.

These amalgams are made
by combining mercury with
silver, tin, and copper. Mercury
makes up about half of the
substance. The mercury binds
all the other metals together
and makes the amalgam hard
and long-lasting.

Using a mercury amalgam
is one of the least expensive
ways to fill a tooth cavity.

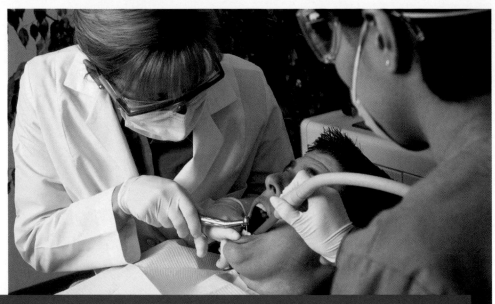

A dentist and her assistant work on a patient. Mercury has been used in dental fillings for many years.

These amalgams have been used for almost 150 years. Studies have shown that the mercury in these amalgams does not pose any danger to humans. Even though mercury may be present in a person's mouth, he or she is likely to be exposed to more mercury in food, air, and water.

Luckily, scientists have discovered a lot about mercury since the 1800s. We know why Alice's Mad Hatter told such strange riddles and we've learned how to prevent mercury poisoning. Perhaps most importantly, we know much more about how we can safely use this element's helpful properties without harming ourselves and our environment.

Fun Facts
About Mercury

- Mercury is also known as quicksilver because it is silver in color and flows quickly.

- A brick, a lump of lead, and a cannonball will all float in liquid mercury.

- Mercury is not magnetic.

- Mercury is thirteen and a half times as heavy as an equal volume of water.

- The element oxygen was discovered when a compound made from mercury and oxygen was heated.

- At one time, people known as alchemists believed that mercury could be changed into gold.

To Find Out More

If you would like to learn more about mercury, check out these additional sources.

 **Books**

Krasnow, David, and Tom Seddon. **Elements.** Gareth Stevens, 2003.

Oxlade, Chris. **Elements & Compounds.** Heinemann Library, 2002.

Stwertka, Albert. **A Guide to Elements.** Oxford University Press, 1996.

Tocci, Salvatore. **The Periodic Table.** Children's Press, 2004.

Watt, Susan. **Mercury.** Benchmark Books, 2004.

Mercury—The Element
http://www.dnr.wi.gov/ org/caer/cea/mercury/ element.htm

Besides providing information about the properties of mercury, this site also describes how mercury gets into the air, soil, and water.

National Geographic
http://news.national geographic.com/news/ 2001/07/0717_lincoln.html

Did Abraham Lincoln suffer from mercury poisoning? Read about how Lincoln took little blue pills for his depression. These pills, which contained mercury, were commonly taken in the 1800s for various conditions.

Mercury and Its Many Forms
http://www.calpoison.org/ public/mercury.html

This site is maintained by the California Poison Action Line and provides a lot of information about mercury poisoning. You can find out which herbal products and folk remedies contain mercury. Information is also provided on how to clean up a mercury spill.

U.S. Environmental Protection Agency
http://www.epa.gov/ mercury/about.htm

Information about mercury is presented along with answers to frequently asked questions. You can also find links to other sites that contain information about mercury.

Important Words

amalgam substance made by mixing mercury with one or more other metals

compound substance formed when two or more different elements are combined

conductor substance through which electricity and heat pass

element building block of matter

matter stuff or material that makes up everything in the universe

microorganism tiny living thing that can only be seen with a microscope

vaporize to turn into a gas

Answers to the riddles on page 4
1. Can I do the filling?   3. Footsteps
2. Your name   4. The letter M

Index

Meet the Author

Salvatore Tocci is a science writer who lives in East Hampton, New York, with his wife, Patti. He was a high school biology and chemistry teacher for almost thirty years. His books include a high school chemistry textbook and an elementary school book series that encourages students to perform experiments to learn about science. Like most people, he never looks forward to having his dentist use a mercury amalgam to fill a tooth cavity.